Cover art: "The Hooded Man," November 4, 2003. This image was taken at Abu Ghraib and later seized by the U.S. government. The prisoner was nicknamed "Gilligan," eventually identified as Abdou Hussain Saad Faleh.

For performance rights please contact:
Youssef Alaoui Fdili (iuoala@gmail.com)
Anton Bonnici (anton@theopiatebooks.com)

ISBN: 978-2-9593278-8-9

© Anton Bonnici & Youssef Alaoui Fdili 2025

"There is no present or future—only the past, happening over and over again—now."
-Eugene O'Neill

"Power does not corrupt men; fools, however, if they get into a position of power, corrupt power."
-George Bernard Shaw

"Jails and prisons are designed to break human beings, to convert the population into specimens in a zoo—obedient to our keepers, but dangerous to each other. In response, imprisoned men and women will invent and continually invoke various and sundry defenses. Consequently, two layers of existence can be encountered within almost every jail or prison."
-Angela Davis

When The Phone Rang

A One Act Play

Adapted for the stage by
Anton Bonnici & Youssef Alaoui

from the short story by
Youssef Alaoui

Foreword by
Genna Rivieccio

Contents

Foreword 1

The Play 5

The Short Story 79

Afterword 113

Foreword

"The *because* doesn't matter anymore." So Muhammad tells us shortly into the play version of "When the Phone Rang," after we see him being interrogated by an American soldier. The "because" *never* mattered, of course. There has *never* been a true rhyme or reason to discrimination at its most vile. Other than for those in power to weaponize fear, to use it as a tool for control over the masses. And while one might have thought that the masses would have gotten "wise" to this tactic by now, it appears they are more susceptible to it than ever.

Youssef Alaoui's short story, "When the Phone Rang," was first published in *The Opiate* in 2019, during the final dregs of the Trump presidency. Or what would turn out merely to be the *first* Trump presidency. Even though it appeared that, by 2020, everybody, even the staunchest of Republicans, had learned their lesson about throwing support behind someone so ignominious. Apparently, though, Americans (and, more specifically, American politicians) no longer have any aversion whatsoever to ignominy, willingly electing the Orange One (more willingly, in fact, than they did in 2016) in lieu of "letting" a woman, least of all a woman of color, into the highest office in the land. She wasn't "qualified" enough. Whereas a convicted felon/rapist who has been failing upward his entire life somehow is.

Where once it seemed as though George W. Bush was the apex of incompetency in the annals of U.S. presidencies, he has since been made to look like a saintly genius compared to the person currently running the show. And it *is* just that to him: a show, a spectacle, something to "drum up ratings." He is, after all, the "reality TV" president. Even so, that he could have the audacity to tell Volodymyr Zelenskyy, during what has now become an illustrious televised meeting, "This is gonna be great television, I will say that" still invoked a sickening feeling in the pit of one's stomach. Regardless of how we've all been conditioned by now to be surprised by nothing. Certainly not the grotesque.

When Alaoui's short story was published at the end of the 2010s, theoretically, everyone should have "moved on" from the horrors of the 00s period when initial reports of what was happening at Guantánamo were swirling. This in addition to the reports of how Americans should be terrified of anyone associated with Islam. In other words, the message was: fear all Middle Eastern people. And in the wake of 9/11, the liberty with which racial profiling was able to flourish knew no bounds. Carte blanche was given to the U.S. government a.k.a. George W. Bush (and his overlord, Dick Cheney) by the American people themselves. And oh, how that government ran with it. Just as they are running with it now.

The only difference, as many have already pointed out, is that, this time around, the mask is fully off. No pretending on the government's part that they aren't what they are: fascists here to subjugate. To oppress. To deport. To torture. And not only that, to profit from it immensely. At another moment toward the end of the play, Muhammad asks, "Why should I relax when my life is spiraling down the drain? When it is a risk to my life to walk home with bread while being Arabic? Why should I relax when it is forbidden to go here or there while being from somewhere else? Why must I live my life out in this cage of racial profiling, because of someone else's paranoid determination?"

There will probably never be an answer that can satisfy those who have endured the results of such "paranoid determination," to put it mildly. Though the answer is, in a nutshell, that every form of government, across millennia, has needed a scapegoat. A group of people to blame for their own shortcomings. In the end, that government's frailties have always come to light. But that doesn't mean that irreparable damage was not done (and is not still *being* done) while the American people were sleeping. Waking up intermittently, only to fall right back asleep again, obstinately blind to what their elected officials are doing, the lives they are destroying. All in the name of "keeping the peace," of course. And though Karl Marx may have said, "History repeats itself, first as a tragedy, second as a farce," none of what's happening/repeating right now feels very fucking funny.

Genna Rivieccio
Editor, The Opiate Books
Spring 2025

The Play

CHARACTERS:

MUHAMMAD – a prisoner of war, mid-forties

PRISONER MUHAMMAD – a body stand-in for MUHAMMAD

TWO AMERICAN SOLDIERS – both in their early twenties

SCALDED FACE/SHADOWY FIGURE/ABDELAZIZ – a mysterious persona with a scalded face and a raspy voice

FIVE TO SIX REBEL SOLDIERS – a group of rag-tag guerrillas

NOTE: SOLDIERS can be either male or female.

NOTES:

The set is comprised of three areas:

The SANCTUARY – a domestic living room set across the upper sections of the stage and center stage.

The INTERROGATION OFFICE – an area placed downstage right.

The HOLDING CELL – an area placed downstage left.

The SANCTUARY set is humble. A couch at the back of the stage with a record player on a set of drawers next to it, and a small 1980s/1990s-era TV on a short TV unit at the center facing the couch, facing away from the audience. The couch needs to be raised as such so that the actor sitting is easily visible. Next to the TV, on the TV unit, is a wired home rotary telephone set. To the left of the couch, upstage left, is a rolled-up carpet in a small prayer area.

The INTERROGATION OFFICE has a metal table with two metal chairs across each other. The table has a metal bar running along the side with handcuffs hanging. There's a bucket underneath the table and a small lamp on it. Files and documents can be seen organized on the table next to the lamp.

The HOLDING CELL is represented by a raised platform on wheels that may be moved around the stage or offstage when needed. Fixed on the platform is a metal construction that represents a cuboid cage, with one entire back wall of bars and the remaining three walls incomplete and open with just enough corners and edges to give the impression of a full cube. Handcuffs on a chain run through a loop on the floor and a black box is affixed to the top of the cage with cables attached to it.

The back wall of the stage, above the couch, is a projection screen. A variety of projections will be used throughout the performance.

SCENE 01

LIGHTS UP ON:

INTERROGATION OFFICE

MUHAMMAD is sitting on a chair across from SOLDIER ONE at the interrogation table. MUHAMMAD has his hands handcuffed to the table in front of him. SOLDIER ONE is holding a folder and looking at documents under the lamplight. SOLDIER TWO is standing behind SOLDIER ONE.

{ITALICS in ARABIC}

SOLDIER ONE: *Is your name Muhammad?*

MUHAMMAD: *Yes.*

SOLDIER ONE: *Are you the son of Mr. and Mrs. Nablus?*

MUHAMMAD: *Yes.*

SOLDIER ONE: *Is your mobile phone number 00964630042?*

MUHAMMAD: *Yes.*

SOLDIER ONE: *Do you live on al-Mutanabbi Street?*

MUHAMMAD: *Yes, I do.*

{CONTINUING IN ENGLISH}

SOLDIER ONE: Do you work at the old medina downtown?

MUHAMMAD: Yes, I do. The souk.

SOLDIER ONE: Since when have you worked there?

MUHAMMAD: Fifteen years.

SOLDIER ONE: And what did you do before then?

MUHAMMAD: I was a baker's apprentice. I worked at Paradise Bakery.

SOLDIER ONE: Have you ever traveled to Egypt?

MUHAMMAD: No.

SOLDIER ONE: Has any relative of yours ever traveled to Egypt or Afghanistan?

MUHAMMAD: Not that I remember.

SOLDIER ONE: Do you know anyone at all, a neighbor, or friend or acquaintance, that has ever traveled to Egypt?

MUHAMMAD: No. Not that I know.

SOLDIER ONE: Have you ever used a firearm?

MUHAMMAD: Never.

SOLDIER ONE: Have you ever received any training in the use of firearms?

MUHAMMAD: No. Never.

SOLDIER ONE: Have you ever handled materials for the assembly of explosive devices?

MUHAMMAD: No. Not that I know.

SOLDIER ONE: Have you ever received any training in the assembly of explosive devices?

MUHAMMAD: No.

SOLDIER ONE: Have you ever researched online or asked others online for instructions or information about the assembly of explosive devices?

MUHAMMAD: No, never.

SOLDIER ONE: Do you know anyone who has in their possession illegal firearms or explosive devices?

MUHAMMAD: No, I don't.

SOLDIER ONE: Do you know anyone who is planning to use illegal firearms or explosive devices to commit an act of terror?

MUHAMMAD: No, I don't.

SOLDIER ONE: Do you know anyone who has ever committed an act of terror using illegal firearms or explosive devices?

MUHAMMAD: No, I don't.

SOLDIER ONE: Do you know anyone who is planning to or has financed the purchase of illegal firearms or explosive devices for use in a terrorist plot?

MUHAMMAD: No, I don't know anyone with such plans or resources.

SOLDIER ONE: Have you ever received training in terrorist activities?

MUHAMMAD: No, I haven't.

SOLDIER ONE: Have you ever been involved in plotting an act of terror?

MUHAMMAD: No, I haven't.

SOLDIER ONE: Do you know anyone who has called for violence on American soil and promoted jihad?

MUHAMMAD: No, I don't.

SOLDIER ONE: Have you ever called for violence on American soil and promoted jihad?

MUHAMMAD: No, I haven't. Never.

SOLDIER ONE: Have you ever become aware of suspicious activity that may have led to an act of terror on American soil?

MUHAMMAD: No, never.

SOLDIER ONE: On the seventh of November at four p.m., were you walking down Yazidi Street?

MUHAMMAD: Yes. That's the day you picked me up.

SOLDIER ONE: What were you carrying?

MUHAMMAD: Bread.

SOLDIER ONE: Only bread?

MUHAMMAD: Only bread.

SOLDIER ONE: What were your intentions that day?

MUHAMMAD: Eat bread.

SOLDIER ONE: On seventh of November at four p.m., you were walking down Yazidi Street on your way home to eat bread?

MUHAMMAD: Yes.

SOLDIER ONE: Were you aware that, not less than two hundred meters from your location, on Yazidi Street, a squad of soldiers was attacked by an explosive device?

MUHAMMAD: I was not.

SOLDIER ONE: And are you aware now?

MUHAMMAD: Yes.

SOLDIER ONE: How did you become aware?

MUHAMMAD: You told me.

SOLDIER ONE: So, before I made you aware of this information, you had no idea that, two hundred meters away from your location on Yazidi Street, a squad of soldiers had just been attacked by an explosive device?

MUHAMMAD: I had no idea. I was walking home with bread.

SOLDIER ONE: Did you have anything to do with the setting of that explosive device?

MUHAMMAD: No. Nothing.

SOLDIER ONE: Were you aware of any plans to use said explosive device?

MUHAMMAD: No. None at all.

SOLDIER ONE: Do you have information about others with the means to purchase or construct such explosive device?

MUHAMMAD: I do not.

SOLDIER ONE: Did you take any pleasure when you became aware of this attack?

MUHAMMAD: Not at all.

SOLDIER ONE: Do you know anyone who might have taken pleasure in seeing this act of war committed?

MUHAMMAD: No.

SOLDIER ONE: Have you been in the company of someone you could have taken pleasure with in seeing this act of war committed?

MUHAMMAD: No, I have never been in such company, and I have never taken such pleasure.

SOLDIER ONE: What did you feel when you became aware of this attack?

MUHAMMAD: Fear.

SOLDIER ONE: Why were you afraid?

MUHAMMAD: Because I abhor violence and I know that violence only creates more violence. I know that these acts only bring more pain and destruction and not peace. This is why I was afraid.

LIGHTS DIM.

SCENE 02

LIGHTS UP ON:

HOLDING CELL

SOLDIER ONE and SOLDIER TWO are holding MUHAMMAD against the iron bars on the HOLDING CELL PLATFORM. They put him in a squatting position, they cuff both his ankles to one of the lower bars, then they pass both his hands from underneath his crotch and handcuff both hands to another knee-high bar. Finally, SOLDIER ONE takes a BLACK HOOD out of his pocket and dresses MUHAMMAD with it. SOLDIER ONE and SOLDIER TWO exit the stage. A few seconds of silence with MUHAMMAD in a spot of light before the VOICEOVER narration starts.

MUHAMMAD (V.O.): These are the years between the wars. Toward the end of the last war, I was plucked from the streets of my town because I was walking home with bread on the wrong day. Because the black smoke blew south rather than north. Because invading forces mistook themselves for rebel forces. Because rebel forces mistook themselves for allied forces. Because the crusaders were in fact supporters. Because a gunnery sergeant spoke like Yosemite Sam.

Because that sergeant howled and gesticulated from his perch, farting out last night's Spam chili in the back of a truck picking off *Hajjis* and then he shot a little boy, after the boy had shooed his sister home on her bicycle. The *because* doesn't matter anymore. I have been detained in the same manner as any other enemy combatant, if they are not killed on sight. It is well within the broad and permissive guidelines defining enemy combatants, as they are wont to flex and shake like the disco shorts of a midnight cowgirl, snapping her gum and smiling on the cell phone behind the bushes, under the stairwell of military protocol, commingling with bloodlust and prescription-addled shellshock.

As the last few lines are being heard in VOICEOVER, MUHAMMAD starts removing his shackles. First, he uncuffs his hands, then he lowers himself to uncuff his ankles and, finally, he removes the hood from his face which he holds in his hands to show to the audience. Once he is free, he continues to deliver his monologue to the audience in person. The transition from VOICEOVER to LIVE PERFORMANCE should be seamless.

MUHAMMAD (LIVE): *(in Arabic)* My name is Muhammad. *(in English)* My name is Muhammad. I have been chained to a concrete floor in a stress position for four days. This is the fifteenth such session in my broad career as a prisoner for the past four years. My knees feel like railroad pikes have been sledgehammered down through the marrow. My eyes feel like they weep blood, and my teeth are folding in on themselves, or maybe the entire thing is an illusion, but the feelings are convincing enough to make me believe that I will never die, but that I would, in fact, see heaven unfold before me right here in my cell, shitting myself, chained to the floor; viewing it glow through my hood, to the tune of the music playing through the speakers above. Inside that selfsame hood, I have carefully traced out the lines of tree-filled windows with my mind's eye.

Music is heard softly and projected on the wall behind the couch. We can see a line being traced in white chalk on the blackness. A large window is drawn. Once the outline is complete, the window opens outwards and a clear blue sky appears with a green landscape of hills and trees in the distance. Soft, billowing curtains appear on the sides of the window and a soft light shines on the living room set.

MUHAMMAD (CONT'D): My windows are dressed with blowing curtains and mounted in walls of flowery wall paper. The ringing in my ears is birds chirping by day and crickets by night. I tap my thighs in remembrance to the drumbeats of my youth, now burned and stamped out like rank cigarettes made of chewing gum paper stuffed with camel dung.

I have no further hope of returning home. My new home is dark, but well-lit within the universe I have created. My couch is soft. My floor is thick with rugs. My record player works. My television is boring. Delightfully boring and irrelevant. I sit against the couch on the floor and gaze for hours at the shifting images on my black and white television set. Egyptian movies from the 1950s and 60s stream endlessly. Oum Kalthoum sings to full auditoriums with her arms out wide, sound emanating from her chest, the core of her love, as I doze lightly, deep in the summery afternoons of the galaxy behind my black hood.

Video samples of vintage black and white Egyptian movies and of Oum Kalthoum in concert are projected on the screen as he is mentioning them. MUHAMMAD is enjoying the singing, with his own arms outstretched like Kalthoum. As the singing rises in volume, we start hearing the ringing of a phone. MUHAMMAD notices the ringing and switches off the TV. Then he looks at the ringing phone for a couple of seconds without approaching it. The phone stops ringing. MUHAMMAD looks at the phone, astonished.

BLACKOUT.

SCENE 03

LIGHTS UP ON:

INTERROGATION OFFICE

MUHAMMAD is sitting on a chair across from SOLDIER ONE at the interrogation table, with his hands cuffed to the table. SOLDIER ONE is holding a folder and looking at documents under the lamplight. SOLDIER TWO is standing behind SOLDIER ONE.

SOLDIER ONE: Is your name Muhammad?

MUHAMMAD: Yes.

SOLDIER ONE: Are you the son of Mr. and Mrs. Nablus?

MUHAMMAD: Yes.

SOLDIER ONE: Is your mobile phone number 00964630042?

MUHAMMAD:	Yes.
SOLDIER ONE:	Do you live on al-Mutanabbi Street?
MUHAMMAD:	Yes, I do.
SOLDIER ONE:	Do you work at the souk downtown?
MUHAMMAD:	Yes, I do.
SOLDIER ONE:	How long have you worked there?
MUHAMMAD:	Fifteen years.
SOLDIER ONE:	And what did you do before then?
MUHAMMAD:	I was a baker's apprentice. I worked at Paradise Bakery.
SOLDIER ONE:	Have you ever traveled to Egypt?
MUHAMMAD:	No.
SOLDIER ONE:	Has any relative of yours ever traveled to Egypt?
MUHAMMAD:	Not that I remember.

SOLDIER ONE: Do you know anyone at all, a neighbor, or friend or acquaintance, that has ever traveled to Egypt or Afghanistan?

MUHAMMAD: I do not.

SOLDIER ONE: Have you ever used a firearm?

MUHAMMAD: Never.

SOLDIER ONE: Have you ever received any training in the use of firearms?

MUHAMMAD: No. Never.

SOLDIER ONE: Have you ever handled materials for the assembly of explosive devices?

MUHAMMAD: No.

SOLDIER ONE: Have you ever received any training into the assembly of explosive devices?

MUHAMMAD: No.

SOLDIER ONE: Have you ever researched online or asked others online for instructions or information about the assembly of explosive devices?

MUHAMMAD: No, never.

SOLDIER ONE: Do you know anyone who owns illegal firearms or explosive devices?

MUHAMMAD: I do not.

SOLDIER ONE: Have you ever acquired illegal firearms or explosive devices to be used by rebel forces?

MUHAMMAD: No, I haven't.

SOLDIER ONE: Do you know anyone who is involved in military operations carried out by rebel forces?

MUHAMMAD: No, I don't.

SOLDIER ONE: Do you know anyone who is planning to or has financed the purchase of firearms or explosive devices for use by rebel forces?

MUHAMMAD: No, I don't know anyone with such plans or resources.

SOLDIER ONE: Have you ever received military training by rebel forces?

MUHAMMAD: No, I have not.

SOLDIER ONE: Have you ever been involved in rebel activity?

MUHAMMAD: No.

SOLDIER ONE: Do you know anyone who has called for violence on American soil and promoted jihad?

MUHAMMAD: No.

SOLDIER ONE: Have you ever called for violence on American soil and promoted jihad?

MUHAMMAD: No, I haven't. Never.

SOLDIER ONE: Have you ever become aware of suspicious activity that may have led to rebel activity on foreign soil?

MUHAMMAD: No, never.

SOLDIER ONE: Are you aware that acts of warfare are being perpetrated in Iraq and Afghanistan?

MUHAMMAD: I am aware.

SOLDIER ONE: Where were you on the seventh of November at exactly four p.m.?

MUHAMMAD: I was walking down Yazidi Street carrying bread.

SOLDIER ONE: And where were you exactly one hour before then?

MUHAMMAD: I was at home.

SOLDIER ONE: What were you doing at home?

MUHAMMAD: Taking a nap.

SOLDIER ONE: And how did you end up in the street carrying bread an hour later?

MUHAMMAD: I woke up from my nap, my wife was making dinner, so I went out to get some bread.

SOLDIER ONE: Did you see anyone suspicious on your way to get bread?

MUHAMMAD: No.

SOLDIER ONE: Where did you get your bread from?

MUHAMMAD: From Mr. al-Qadam down the street.

SOLDIER ONE: What did you and Mr. *(hesitates on pronunciation)* al-Qadam talk about?

MUHAMMAD: Nothing.

SOLDIER ONE: You did not talk to Mr. al-Qadam?

MUHAMMAD: I talked to him but only to get my bread. "I want some bread, here's your money," et cetera. We did not talk about anything in particular.

SOLDIER ONE: Did Mr. al-Qadam say something suspicious or act suspiciously when he sold you the bread?

MUHAMMAD: No. He just sold me the bread; I took the bread and I left.

SOLDIER ONE: Do you always buy your bread from Mr. al-Qadam?

MUHAMMAD: Yes. He is near my home.

SOLDIER ONE: Have you ever heard or seen Mr. al-Qadam say or do something suspicious?

MUHAMMAD: Never.

SOLDIER ONE: Do you think Mr. al-Qadam has any knowledge in the construction and use of explosive devices?

MUHAMMAD: I don't know. I don't think so.

SOLDIER ONE: If you don't know, why don't you think so?

MUHAMMAD: Because he is not the type.

SOLDIER ONE: What type?

MUHAMMAD: The military type, the violent type, someone who would be constructing bombs to kill people.

SOLDIER ONE: And if Mr. al-Qadam was the type, you'd be able to recognize it?

MUHAMMAD: I don't know. I can't be sure. All I know is that I've known Mr. al-Qadam for fifteen years and I have never, ever heard him say a single word inciting or wishing or planning any form of violence on anyone, be it local or foreign.

SOLDIER ONE: And that makes you think he could not have been involved in the setting of an explosive device that killed a squad of six American soldiers on routine surveillance duty?

MUHAMMAD: Yes, I honestly believe Mr. al-Qadam had nothing to do with that.

SOLDIER ONE: Do you know anyone who might have had something to do with that?

MUHAMMAD: I do not.

SOLDIER ONE: And if you knew anyone who might have had something to do with that, would you tell us about him?

MUHAMMAD: Yes, I would. I would tell you everything. But I know nothing. I swear.

SOLDIER ONE: If you had the information, why would you help us?

MUHAMMAD: Because I want all of this to be over.

SOLDIER ONE: This what?

MUHAMMAD: The war.

SOLDIER ONE: Why would you want the war to be over?

MUHAMMAD: Because I don't want to live in war, and I'm afraid for the life of my loved ones.

LIGHTS DIM.

SCENE 04

LIGHTS UP ON:

HOLDING CELL

SOLDIER ONE and SOLDIER TWO are holding MUHAMMAD against the iron bars on the HOLDING CELL PLATFORM. They put him in a squatting position, they cuff both his ankles to one of the lower bars, then they pass both his hands from underneath his crotch and handcuff both hands to another knee-high bar. Finally, SOLDIER ONE takes a BLACK HOOD out of his pocket and lowers it over the head of MUHAMMAD. SOLDIER ONE and SOLDIER TWO exit the stage. A few seconds of silence with MUHAMMAD in a spotlight before the projection of the window with the blue skies and the landscape view reappears. MUHAMMAD uncuffs himself and removes the BLACK HOOD.

MUHAMMAD: Corporeal pain is the last thing that ties me to this world. It confines me like a shipyard rope, tight against my midriff, squeezing out the final drops of my humanity. My tears will not spill forth. My eyes drip something slowly, more viscous than tears, which I assume is blood. The muscles in my face are also cramped and bleeding, for they are locked into position as the rest of my body. The guards do not let me stand nor sleep, but I'm removed from my cage daily for prayers and questioning. I have no ideas. I have no opinions. One day I'm asked about the terror attack on so and so. The next I'm asked if I know this or that rebel group. The questions keep coming, each round more surreal than the next. I have no ideas. I have no opinions. I know a few people. Those people are doing their business. I do not want their business. What I do want is the guards dead and everything around me destroyed. I hate the invaders and I pray for vengeance as I feel myself slowly dying in my cell. I call out in my brain to Allah to come visit and take me away, but he does not come. I am alone. I live out my days in the room inside my hood, keeping my eyes on the windows, watching the trees move beyond them.

I'm pretty sure I heard that phone ring. It did, didn't it? But how can that be? How can the phone inside my hood ring without me willing it to? I must be controlling this somehow. Next time, I will be ready to pick it up.

*The phone starts ringing, and MUHAMMAD picks it up. We hear morse code—*bip bip boop bip boop boop boop—*and then silence. MUHAMMAD puts the phone down.*

MUHAMMAD (CONT'D): It sounds like Morse code! I remember Morse code from my school days. For a time, it was a fascination of mine, a compulsion where, as I listened to my favorite music, I tried to match the lyrics spelled out in Morse code to the rhythm of the song. And this message is surely in Morse code, but it takes me by surprise. I have already forgotten its beats; I have to hear it again. But, more importantly, who could be calling? Who could be calling me here on my imaginary phone? Who would have the number to the inside of my head? It must be God. Surely this is some kind of divine intervention. Maybe God is finally going to visit and thought he would be considerate enough to call first to clarify matters…perhaps there are conditions that I should know about. Any good scholar knows that God has plenty of conditions for pilgrims on their way to heaven.

In that case, I thank my lucky stars and I will make sure I take the time to think about the phone call for the next three days. Here! I will also change the position of the phone. Now it is closer to the couch where I spend most of my time, so I can more easily talk on the phone and gaze dreamily out the windows, or maybe we can talk about the programs I'm watching on the television. Yes, it must be closer so I can answer it quickly, perhaps by the first ring, like this.

(imitating the telephone ring) Rrrrrrrhello! Yes, this is Muhammad! God? I have been waiting for so long to hear from you. Yes, I would be so overwhelmed with joy to live with you in your kingdom. Yes, I have kept to the five pillars. No, no cheating or lying. I am good to my fellow men. And women! I am kind to my mother! No, no masturbation. No. I am sorry. That time was an accident. Thank you for understanding, God. God you are merciful! God you are great!

I will wait for God to call again. And I will pray.

MUHAMMAD unrolls his prayer rug and shows it to the audience. It has a little compass embedded in its top.

MUHAMMAD (CONT'D): When I was still free, when I was still a human, I brought a travel prayer rug with me when I was away from home. My father gave it to me before he passed. It was already used. *(sad laugh)* I thought it was silly at the time. *Look here: {in ARABIC}* it has its own small compass here on top so I'm always sure I'm facing Mecca. Here, in the world traced inside my hood, the compass will sometimes spin for a few minutes. This is the domain of non-reality, or perhaps this is SUPER-REALITY. I am transfixed by the magic. I stare at it and try to feel the magnetic poles blowing past me like storm clouds, or maybe it's Mecca on a train or, better yet, maybe the compass needle follows the Kaaba which has escaped on a flying carpet to avoid the fundamentalists of the world, turning the compass round and around.

Projection of a spinning compass in a cloudy sky. MUHAMMAD finds his direction when the compass stops spinning, and he sets the prayer rug down. He kneels in his praying position on the rug and is just about to pray when the phone rings again. He hesitates. The phone rings again. MUHAMMAD leaps to answer it, but when he answers, there's only a dial tone.

MUHAMMAD (CONT'D): Hello?

There's no reply. The audience can still hear the tone. Then MUHAMMAD looks at the phone and holds down the button on its cradle as if the phone has been put down. It rings immediately and he lifts his finger off in reaction.

(phone rings)

MUHAMMAD: Hello?

Bip bip boop bip boop boop boop.

MUHAMMAD: Sorry?

Boop boop bip bip boop.

MUHAMMAD: And…nothing. So, I hang up. I think about the combination of short and long pulses for the rest of the day. *Bip bip boop bip boop boop boop* followed by *boop boop bip bip boop*. So odd. I begin to think to myself in Morse code. I spell out every thought, every concept, everything that enters my mind for that afternoon in Morse code.

As he is saying this, we see a video animation inside the window frame: animated lines of thought turning into dashes and dots in Morse. Questions and phrases like: Is God talking to me? How long have I been in here? Am I ready to receive Allah? I have kept to the five pillars! I am kind to my mother! I hate the invaders... They appear in words and morph into Morse code with corresponding sounds.

MUHAMMAD (CONT'D): It takes me the entire following day to correctly spell my thoughts on the matter. I gaze at myself in the bathroom mirror *(of his fantasy apartment, not in the prison cell)*, I bow and rinse my face. *Boop boop bip bip boop*, I keep repeating when the inkling of an understanding edges in upon me.

(in Arabic) OH SHIT! *(in English)* No! It can't be! *(holds head in hands)* How silly. Is this how God chooses to communicate?

MUHAMMAD grabs a pen and a paper from a drawer and goes to the couch. We can see what he is writing on the paper projected on the screen above him in the window frame: Kif 7alik shu 3am ta3mil - (Howzzit goin wassup).

MUHHAMAD: Allah speaks Arabish text slang?

MUHAMMAD looks perplexed.

BLACKOUT.

SCENE 05

LIGHTS UP ON:

INTERROGATION OFFICE

MUHAMMAD is seated on a chair across from SOLDIER ONE and has his hands cuffed to the table in front of him. SOLDIER ONE is holding a folder and looking at documents under the lamplight. SOLDIER TWO is standing right in front of MUHAMMAD and, throughout the entire interrogation, after every single answer that MUHAMMAD gives, SOLDIER TWO slaps him hard in the face.

SOLDIER ONE: Is your name Muhammad?

MUHAMMAD: Yes.

SLAP.

SOLDIER ONE: Are you the son of Mr. and Mrs. Nablus?

MUHAMMAD: Yes.

SLAP.

SOLDIER ONE: Is your mobile phone number 00964630042?

MUHAMMAD: Yes.

SLAP.

SOLDIER ONE: Do you live on al-Mutanabbi Street?

MUHAMMAD: Yes.

SLAP.

SOLDIER ONE: Do you work at your privately-owned booth in the souk?

MUHAMMAD: Yes.

SLAP.

SOLDIER ONE: Since when have you worked there?

MUHAMMAD: Over fifteen years!

SLAP.

SOLDIER ONE: And what did you do before then?

MUHAMMAD: Baker's. Apprentice.

SLAP.

SOLDIER ONE: Have you ever traveled to Afghanistan?

MUHAMMAD: No.

SLAP.

SOLDIER ONE: Has any relative of yours ever traveled to Afghanistan?

MUHAMMAD: No.

SLAP.

SOLDIER ONE: Do you know anyone at all, a neighbor, or friend or acquaintance, that has ever traveled to Afghanistan?

MUHAMMAD: No.

SLAP.

SOLDIER ONE: Have you ever used a firearm?

MUHAMMAD: No.

SLAP.

At this point, the interrogation freezes, SOLDIER ONE and TWO stop mid-movement, and MUHAMMAD leaves his chair and addresses the audience.

MUHAMMAD: Not even these interrogations can distract me from thinking about what the code has revealed. I still can't believe what I have written. "Howzzit goin wassup?" Is that really how God speaks? Could God be playing a trick on me? Or perhaps it is part of my torture. Somehow, the guards have found a way to enter my sanctuary. Now I wish for death. I no longer wish to be visited by God. The last thing I need is to be visited by an asshole prison guard dressed up like God, if that could possibly be done, but if they were faking God, then why not fake godly speaking? Why would Allah, praised be his name, choose to communicate with me in that manner? The questions are unending, and I don't know how long I can endure these tortured thoughts before my mind dissolves completely.

MUHAMMAD takes his place back on the chair and the interrogation continues.

SOLDIER ONE: Have you ever been trained in the use of firearms?

MUHAMMAD: No.

SLAP.

SOLDIER ONE: Have you ever handled materials for the assembly of explosive devices?

MUHAMMAD: No.

SLAP.

SOLDIER ONE: Have you ever received training into the assembly of explosive devices?

MUHAMMAD: No.

SLAP.

SOLDIER ONE: Have you ever researched online or asked others online for instructions or information about the assembly of explosive devices?

MUHAMMAD: No.

SLAP.

SOLDIER ONE: Do you know anyone who has in their possession illegal firearms or explosive devices?

MUHAMMAD: No. I don't.

SLAP.

SOLDIER ONE: Do you know anyone who is planning to use illegal firearms and explosive devices to commit an act of terror?

MUHAMMAD: No.

SLAP.

The lights fade to BLACK and we hear the next three questions and answers in the darkness, with the voices lowering in volume, fading out, after which there is silence.

SOLDIER ONE: Do you know anyone who has ever committed an act of terror using illegal firearms and explosive devices?

MUHAMMAD: No.

SLAP.

SOLDIER ONE: Do you know anyone who is planning to or has financed the purchase of illegal firearms and explosive devices for the use in a terrorist plot?

MUHAMMAD: No.

SLAP.

SOLDIER ONE: Have you ever received training in terrorist activity?

MUHAMMAD: No.

SLAP.

BLACKOUT.

SCENE 06

LIGHTS UP ON:

HOLDING CELL & SANCTUARY

SOLDIERS ONE & TWO hold PRISONER MUHAMMAD upright against the bars. The BLACK HOOD is already on him. They cuff his ankles to a lower bar. Then they bend him over ninety degrees from his hips and put his arms behind his back. They handcuff his arms together and then they tie a rope to the chain of the handcuffs. SOLDIER

ONE throws the rope over the cage structure and SOLDIER TWO grabs the rope from the other side. Then they pull the rope, lifting PRISONER MUHAMMAD from his arms as both arms twist and rise backwards. Finally, both SOLDIERS exit. As all of this is happening, MUHAMMAD is on the couch watching himself being tortured; the psychic split is now complete. Once he's alone, he approaches himself in his prison.

MUHAMMAD: I cannot remember how many days have passed. Two. Five. A dozen. I pass my time breathing. I practice breathing slowly, so slowly, almost not breathing at all. I hold tight to my jumpsuit. I feel the fabric against my skin. I make myself aware of the sandals wrapping my feet. I feel my breath entering the duct in my hood. Inside my hood, I relax in my cozy apartment and watch television, in and out of sleep, lounging mindlessly for a good, long time as the curtains move in the windows.

The open window projection reappears. Everything that will be described next by MUHAMMAD will also appear in the projection. The details need to be accurate and harrowing.

MUHAMMAD (CONT'D): Then, suddenly, I notice a face slowly rising outside the window. It has a mostly bald forehead with one long wisp of hair, moving with the breeze. It is the head of a man. The man has been seriously charred on the head. He is not balding: this is all that is left of his scalp. Parts of his skull show through his skin. One eye is missing. Most of his nose is missing. The man smiles, but then half of his face is gone. His teeth are exposed. He can't help but smile. My heart leaps out of my shirt.

Onstage, MUHAMMAD freezes in a look of terror, still hanging in the stress position. We can see PRISONER MUHAMMAD becoming very agitated as the now giant SCALDED FACE looks at him from the projected window frame. PRISONER MUHAMMAD starts breathing heavily, and we can see his hood bursting in and out as he hyperventilates and sucks in air. Finally, MUHAMMAD shouts onstage through his hood:

MUHAMMAD: What the devil!

The SCALDED FACE replies.

SCALDED FACE: No. Not the devil!

With that, the face fades. The light dims on the HOLDING CELL, and now there is only MUHAMMAD onstage.

MUHAMMAD: This can't be a trick. The guards do not have the wherewithal to enter my mind in such a manner. Or do they? It is obviously some sort of trick, but nothing like I have experienced before in my exhaustive prison career. Could there be a drug in the water they used on me the other day? Was that yesterday, or two days ago? I can't remember. Maybe it was three days ago. I try to become present in my prison cell. I try to remember what my cage feels like, what it smells like. It is difficult to remember. Inside my sanctuary *(MUHAMMAD adopts a squatting stress position)*, I take the stress position of my physical body, it is very painful. I can't manage it longer than five minutes. I have to rest, but there is no way to sleep it off. The man in the window stated clearly that he is not the devil. But the devil is known to lie!

The phone rings again. MUHAMMAD doesn't pick it up and continues with his narrative as the phone keeps rising in volume and MUHAMMAD becomes more and more agitated.

MUHAMMAD: That damned phone! Wherever did it come from? I hate it! I do not want to pick it up. It rings for five minutes. Then it rings for an hour. Then the phone rings for the rest of the day. My brain, my sweet and soft brain that has held up so well for four years of punishment, is now finding that its supporting timbers are no more than wet rags at the core. The entire structure of my elaborate, life-giving scaffolding is beginning to rot into a stew; a tagine made of rifle butts and missile tips, bullet holes and jail bars, a concoction soaked with anger, resentment and hatred.

MUHAMMAD picks up the phone. He is agitated.

MUHAMMAD: Hello?

A dim light switches on the INTERROGATION OFFICE, a figure in the shadows is on the phone. He talks to MUHAMMAD.

ABDELAZIZ: *Bip bip boop boop boop boop.*

MUHAMMAD: Nooooooo…no no no no no! Not this again!

Silence. We can hear heavy breathing. MUHAMMAD is still, pressing the phone against his ear, waiting for a sound, getting more and more terrified with each passing second. The shadowy figure talks at his own phone.

ABDELAZIZ: You chased me away.

MUHAMMAD: I did not chase you away!

ABDELAZIZ: You called me the devil. You looked at me like I am some kind of madman. Who do you think you are, anyway?

MUHAMMAD: You are not the devil?

ABDELAZIZ: No.

MUHAMMAD: Aaaallah?

ABDELAZIZ: Certainly not.

MUHAMMAD: Then who are you?

ABDELAZIZ: *(tauntingly, followed by maniacal laughter)* I…am…you!

MUHAMMAD's fear and agitation have reached a breaking point and he faints.

BLACKOUT.

SCENE 07

LIGHTS UP ON:

INTERROGATION OFFICE & SANCTUARY

PRISONER MUHAMMAD is tied down on the table, his head hanging beyond the edge, with his face covered by a thin piece of cloth. SOLDIER TWO is pouring water from a bucket on PRISONER MUHAMMAD as PRISONER MUHAMMAD gurgles and sputters under the cloth like he is drowning. Every few seconds, SOLDIER ONE tells SOLDIER TWO to pause and asks PRISONER MUHAMMAD a question. PRISONER MUHAMMAD does not reply, and the process continues. MUHAMMAD is watching from his couch.

SOLDIER ONE: Where are the rebels hiding? Where is the next terror attack going to be? Who are your collaborators?

> Where are your weapons? Who is your leader? Who is financing your operations? When did you last leave the country? What are your targets?

Three or four questions into the waterboarding interrogation, the action freezes. MUHAMMAD addresses the audience as he surveys closely what the SOLDIERS are doing to PRISONER MUHAMMAD.

MUHAMMAD: By now, I can no longer answer their questions, whatever they do to me. All can I think of is that face…that horrid face. I chased him away, he said. Chased him away? I have done no such thing. Who is that? He said, *"I'm you,"* but I know me and that's definitely not me. I am a kind man! I think of others! I respect people's privacy! Where does he come from? Why wouldn't he knock? Why is his head so badly scalded? Does he need a place to sleep? Or medical attention? But how can this be happening inside my head? How did this visitor intrude my sanctuary? Not just a visitor, but a Peeping Tom, a half-exploded Peeping Tom and maybe even an enemy spy. But what enemy spy? I have no enemies. No political enemies anyway. I sold shoes and used watches at the souk on weekends before I was detained. That old bastard, Ali, down at the end of the lane was quite the boorish ass though— but bless his soul, he might have made it out of town or is probably dead, *hamdoullah*, by the grace of God, but not this god. This is no god. This is a character who seems to want to talk despite his grisly appearance. But why me? Why talk to *me*? What do I have to offer? And for some unknown reason, I am afraid of what he might have to say. I am more afraid of him than I am of my interrogators. I can't even hear their questions. I feel the pain they inflict on me, but only as an afterthought, like an echo reverberating along the length of my spine, pulsating at the base of my brain. Whatever it is they do to me, I'm not there. I'm spending every remaining living second sitting on that couch inside my sanctuary, listening to the telephone ring.

By the end of the narration, the phone starts to ring and MUHAMMAD diverts his attention from the interrogation table to the ringing phone. He's anxious, scared. He picks up the phone and sits on the couch holding the phone as it keeps on ringing. The lights go out on the interrogation table.

SCENE 08

LIGHTS STILL ON FROM PREVIOUS SCENE:

SANCTUARY

The phone is still ringing from the ending of the previous scene. MUHAMMAD is seated on the couch, holding the phone in his hands and considering whether to take the call or not. After a few tense seconds of incessant ringing, MUHAMMAD picks up the phone and the disembodied voice of ABDELAZIZ speaks.

MUHAMMAD: Yes?

ABDELAZIZ (V.O.): Yes.

MUHAMMAD: Do not play games with me, please.

ABDELAZIZ (V.O.): This is no game.

MUHAMMAD: Please tell me what you want from me. I have told the guards all that I know. Are you working for them?

ABDELAZIZ (V.O.): By no means am I working for them.

MUHAMMAD: What can I do for you, in the name of Allah?

ABDELAZIZ (V.O.): I am here to help.

MUHAMMAD: Who are you? An angel? Are you Gabriel?

ABDELAZIZ (V.O.): I am many things. I am a prisoner, like you. I was in Auschwitz. I was in the reeducation camps of Vietnam, of China. I have been in the places that have terror scarred into their name. Dubrava, Abu Ghraib. Guantánamo, Gaza.

A collage of images appears on the window showing the places and their horrors as ABDELAZIZ names them. The final image is of PRISONER MUHAMMAD in his HOLDING CELL. The lights come on the HOLDING CELL and what we see on the screen is the same as what is onstage: PRISONER MUHAMMAD is lifted off the ground, tied to a high bar from his hands stretched out behind him.

MUHAMMAD: How?

ABDELAZIZ (V.O.): I am you. I am your pain. I am The Pain. You may call me Abdelaziz.

MUHAMMAD: How did you manage to get locked up in so many prisons?

ABDELAZIZ (V.O.): Think about it some more.

MUHAMMAD: I don't know what to think. Hello?

SILENCE.

MUHAMMAD addresses the audience.

MUHAMMAD: I have no idea what all this means. If they somehow fed me a hallucinogen in the water all those days ago, it surely would have left my system by now. If it is not that, then how could this have happened? Who is torturing who? I must know! Who is Abdelaziz? How could he possibly speak without half a face? But of course, this is a hallucination of my own making. I have lined the inside of my hood with windows and curtains of my design. The phone is mine. Of course. I have made it. I have invented this world, I live in it, I found sanctuary here, and now there is an invader! With a story to tell, perhaps? Perhaps he can answer questions. I'm too tired to ask questions, and the soldiers have already asked *me* all the questions I can possibly answer. I am an empty husk. It seems like days since the invader told me his name. Again, the telephone rings. (*ringing*) If it is myself I am to confront, I suppose I will be a bit more relaxed and prepared.

The telephone rings and MUHAMMAD picks it up. The voice of ABDELAZIZ speaks, disembodied.

MUHAMMAD:	Hey-lo.
ABDELAZIZ (V.O.):	Yes.
MUHAMMAD:	Yes what?
ABDELAZIZ (V.O.):	Are you ready?
MUHAMMAD:	Ready for what?

ABDELAZIZ (V.O.): Are you ready to talk? Are you ready to face me?

MUHAMMAD: Yes. I believe I am.

Instantly, PRISONER MUHAMMAD releases a hand from his shackles, then the other, then he jumps off the bar he's perched on. He approaches MUHAMMAD in the SANCTUARY and he removes his BLACK HOOD. His face is all burnt and deformed, this is ABDELAZIZ. MUHAMMAD is scared, puts the phone down and takes a few steps back.

ABDELAZIZ: Today I have called to tell you that these guards are not the enemy.

MUHAMMAD: Oh.

ABDELAZIZ: Yes. You are to hold them in your heart from now on as if they were your brothers.

MUHAMMAD: No.

ABDELAZIZ: Yes.

MUHAMMAD: Who are you?

ABDELAZIZ: Abdelaziz. I have told you my name.

MUHAMMAD: Are you a soldier? Are you with them? Are you the commanding officer?

ABDELAZIZ: Not at all. I am here with you.

MUHAMMAD: So the soldiers are my brothers, their rifles scratch my back, and the bombs, they are my toys?

ABDELAZIZ: Ha-ha.

MUHAMMAD: "Ha-ha"? Just what do you mean by "ha-ha"? Can you get me out of here?

ABDELAZIZ: Maybe. We might have to wait a bit longer.

MUHAMMAD: Wait for what? Wait for them to run out of ammunition? Wait for them to run out of their despicable manners? Wait for them to run out of the will to control me?

ABDELAZIZ: Please relax.

MUHAMMAD: Why should I relax when my life is spiraling down the drain? When it is a risk to my life to walk home with bread while being Arabic? Why should I relax when it is forbidden to go here or there while being from somewhere else? Why must I live my life out in this cage of racial profiling, because of someone else's paranoid determination?

ABDELAZIZ: They act like that because they are scared. They are terrified.

MUHAMMAD: Oh yes, of course. Because I said "BOO" and they are all now afraid. This is the most terrifying sound I can make: *BOOOOOOOO!!!!!*

ABDELAZIZ: This is the sound of two cultures interfacing. When commerce is no longer sufficient, battles ensue. The cultures collide. Your conservatives versus their conservatives. Trust me. They are compassionate people. They are fascinated by the sound of your language and are also disgusted by it. They fear the sound of your vowels. Your *ayin*. Your *qoph*. They know it is beautiful and yet still they hate it. They find it repulsive. They find your culture revolting yet fascinating. They think about you often. They confuse themselves with an excess of questions, such as: *How can you allow your women to dress like that? How can you run your business like that? How can you waste your natural resources like that?* It is strange to them, and yet, they want to own it. They want to do your things for you, to correct your wrongs. In the same way, your culture finds their culture atrocious and invasive. Their culture is strange to you and your people. You wish they would stop. You think they are silly. But you like their food. They think your food is weird. You want to be in Hollywood with their women. With their women's breasts. With their G-strings and their pasties. With their soft white children, swimming in their pools.

MUHAMMAD: What are you talking about! How can you say such a thing!!! *(unfazed by talk of breasts and G-strings and filled with nationalistic pride)* I love the sound of my language! Their language is void of all meaning! It sounds like someone is kicking the stomach of a dying pig! In heat! Ours is the language of God! Our writing is holy! Our calligraphy! They have nothing like that! And, by the way, why in the name of God did you choose to contact me in Arabish? That mongrel savage language!

ABDELAZIZ: You used to speak it quite often.

MUHAMMAD: What! Me? No!

ABDELAZIZ: To that woman in the burqa with her breasts out. You would ogle. She would chat with you and take your money.

MUHAMMAD: Oh! No, I just happened to find her website. My friend showed me one day. Anyway, I stopped that! Never mind that! She was evil!

ABDELAZIZ: Arabish is the perfect language for you. It represents your base desires, everything that you hate, yet that still fascinates you. This is the source of hatred. Fixation. Kissing cousins. Objectification, power, resistance. So fragile, so close, so disgusted by one another, and yet so attracted.

MUHAMMAD: I was tricked! She took my money for nothing! She was probably in league with the conservative assholes to make a mockery of people like me, the average ones, the moderates! We are ready to live in a modern world! Stuck in the middle of politics and war! Victimized by every side!

ABDELAZIZ: Enough insults. They believe they are protecting the world.

MUHAMMAD: From what? For whom? Okay, tell me, what does it mean when they kill our children and bomb a hospital?

ABDELAZIZ: Why did the chicken cross the road?

MUHAMMAD: Is that supposed to be funny?

ABDELAZIZ: Think about it. What does it mean?

MUHAMMAD: What does what mean?

ABDELAZIZ: They bomb because it is in their nature to bomb. There is no answer. There are a million answers. For a million people.

MUHAMMAD: Oh, then there should be an all out condemnation of Israelis, Jews, Arabs, Palestinians, Greeks, Turks, Russians, every single better-than-thou American… Who am I leaving out? They all throw bombs!

ABDELAZIZ: And they all receive bombs. Why don't you tell me: what does it say about their nature when they kill children and bomb a hospital?

MUHAMMAD: Because if it is in their nature, then it is not about options or politics—it is about their evil nature.

ABDELAZIZ: Bombs are built to kill humans. Bombs have one single function.

MUHAMMAD: Bombs don't kill people. People do.

ABDELAZIZ: Bombs are just bombs. But more importantly, why do people keep building bombs and launching them at other people? Think about why they do it. Please.

MUHAMMAD: I am not talking about people, I am talking about nations! I am not being metaphysical. I am not playing your game.

ABDELAZIZ: Neither am I. Bombs are built to kill and destroy. End of story.

MUHAMMAD: So you are saying they are killers. That it is in their nature to be killers.

ABDELAZIZ: As are you.

MUHAMMAD: I am not talking about our nation.

ABDELAZIZ: Not all of their nation are killers. And not all of your nation are killers.

MUHAMMAD: I am talking about the children in the playground and the hospital. They die playing on the beach. They die by the side of the road.

ABDELAZIZ: I am specifically talking about the warmongers. People are perversely fascinated by charnel. These nations did not take a consensus or vote together to determine where the next bomb would land. There is one man who made that choice.

MUHAMMAD: Oh, I thought they were a democracy.

ABDELAZIZ: War is never a democracy. Peace is perhaps a democracy. At least it feigns democracy. War, a totalitarianism, is sold to a democracy as a temporary "minimal risk/maximum profit" endeavor. The heads of nations convince their public that the bomb attacks are guaranteed to be clean strikes. Backed by cold science. They call their bomb strikes surgical. Don't you get it? Surgical. That's why they aim at hospitals.

MUHAMMAD: Now that was a joke.

ABDELAZIZ: Busted.

MUHAMMAD: And what of the photo of a burned baby held by a crying man in a crowded funeral procession? How am I supposed to process this?

ABDELAZIZ: If you process it, you are involved in the war.

MUHAMMAD: It is unavoidable, the violence is everywhere. In the streets. Film. Photographs. Right before my eyes! So what should I do, slash my wrists?

ABDELAZIZ: If you slash your wrists, you are participating in the exchange of violence.

MUHAMMAD: I don't understand that. My life doesn't belong to you or anyone else. I don't agree with that assessment at all.

ABDELAZIZ: We are locked in a crisis of revenge. Cause and effect.

MUHAMMAD: Okay, well, I guess I can go shopping now.

ABDELAZIZ: Rather than react violently to the violent emotional exchange, we must accept and say the violence stops with me, rather than the violence begins with me, or the violence will be continued by me. Or how about the following: rather than dropping bombs, these nations should get in a bus, drive over to the border of their enemy, ask permission to enter, be allowed to enter and let's say they sit themselves down in a hospital. Then they would gather the people and say to them: "Who among you will slash your wrists, because we are very angry! Not all of us here, but most of us are quite angry. Frankly, a few of us would rather be at home right now, but our bosses, who couldn't make it on this trip, have ordered us to come here to demand that you slash your wrists, because our God is great, or else we will do it for you. Even though we are not a hundred percent interested in slashing your wrists. A few of us would like to, however. About ten of us. Because we would like to get you back for that attack last week. No, it doesn't matter who suffers for our retribution. So, who will step forward? Show us your babies!"

MUHAMMAD: Show us your boobies?

ABDELAZIZ: Ha-ha.

MUHAMMAD: You say nothing about processing your own emotions.

ABDELAZIZ: My emotions were burned away long ago. Here is what I say. The violence stops with me.

EXIT ABDELAZIZ.

MUHAMMAD: Where are you going? Come back here? I'm not done yet! We're not done yet!!

MUHAMMAD picks up the phone and we hear the dial tone. Then he grabs the wire of the phone, pulls it violently out of the wall and throws the phone to the ground, shattering it. The dial tone can still be heard.

SCENE 09

MUHAMMAD looks at the shattered phone, picks up the receiver, examines it, holds it to his head and addresses the audience. Images form in the window as he talks.

MUHAMMAD: I listen to the dial tone until it stops *(dial tone stops)*. Then I listen to the empty line. I imagine a hundred thousand arguments coming through the wire. I imagine the violence and the retribution. I imagine the endless cycle of the violence whirlpool. The vision fills my mind completely, then it fills the very air before me, completely drowning my meager sanctuary, and then it drowns my cell, then it grows larger than the prison. I imagine a whirlpool so wide that the foaming sides are taller than the walls of a city, with trucks, guns and missiles thrown into the fray with entire hospitals, with women in burqas, with women in G-strings, with tattooed muscle men raping and beating them, with tattooed muscle men raping and beating each other, eating chili cheese fries smothered in hummus and olives, drenched in crude oil, mixed with blood, with Black and Brown people getting shot for driving, getting shot minding their own business, getting shot for believing, for getting imprisoned, for getting caught, forgetting where to be found in accordance with the law, with the Koran, with the Bible, with the Haftorah, for speaking the wrong language at the wrong time, in the wrong country.

As MUHAMMAD is speaking and the image of the WHIRLPOOL starts forming on the screen, the SOLDIERS push the platform of the HOLDING CELL center stage behind him, positioning it so it's ready to receive him while facing the audience. As he keeps speaking, the SOLDIERS grab MUHAMMAD and take him to the HOLDING CELL. ABDELAZIZ joins the SOLDIERS and helps them. The SOLDIERS pull MUHAMMAD's arms out to his sides and they connect wires from the black box at the top of the cage to his fingertips on either side. MUHAMMAD continues addressing the audience throughout this action.

MUHAMMAD (CONT'D): I imagine a giant, spinning whirlpool with a tiny, pointed tip at the bottom that is so far down, so dark, so empty, so void of any mass, of any reason, so void of any conviction, a negative space so absorbing, so compelling, that any mortal would be forced to dive towards it should one witness it, the eye of the storm, the crux of the (hollow) void. AND NOW I KNOW THAT THERE WILL ALWAYS be room for one more to fill it!

By the time he's finished his speech, the projected image of the WHIRLPOOL is at full speed, stretching across all of the performance space. Over the torrential sounds of the spinning WHIRLPOOL, the SOLDIERS start shouting absurd questions as they spin the holding cell around and each time MUHAMMAD answers with a very loud ALLAHU AKBAR. ABDELAZIZ joins in holding a BOX with a button in his hands; he is shouting both the questions with the SOLDIERS and the answer with MUHAMMAD. With every answer, ABDELAZIZ pushes the button, electrocuting MUHAMMAD with a loud buzz, accompanied by a strong STROBE LIGHT that flashes.

SOLDIER ONE & ABDELAZIZ: How many times in your life have you eaten hummus?

MUHAMMAD & ABDELAZIZ: ALLAHU AKBAR!

BUZZ.

SOLDIER TWO & ABDELAZIZ: What is your favorite American movie?

MUHAMMAD & ABDELAZIZ: ALLAHU AKBAR!

BUZZ.

SOLDIER ONE & ABDELAZIZ: How many times in your life have you masturbated?

MUHAMMAD & ABDELAZIZ: ALLAHU AKBAR!

BUZZ.

SOLDIER TWO & ABDELAZIZ: Have you ever fucked a goat?

MUHAMMAD & ABDELAZIZ: ALLAHU AKBAR!

BUZZ.

SOLDIER TWO & ABDELAZIZ: Why don't you like superhero movies?

MUHAMMAD & ABDELAZIZ: ALLAHU AKBAR!

As the questioning escalates, so does the sound of the spinning WHIRLPOOL, with everything sinking into its dark core. Distant warfare sounds fade in.

Bombs drop, automatic weapons fire, and the war approaches until the sound becomes a deafening representation of a battle with machine gunfire, people screaming, explosions, cries for help. The SOLDIERS look surprised and terrified at the sounds; they take out handguns and start shooting at invisible attackers on both sides of the stage. ABDELAZIZ removes the wires attached to MUHAMMAD and frees him. Then everything starts to dim, the sounds of gunfire die out, the SOLDIERS are now moving in slow motion, the spinning WHIRLPOOL swallows itself into darkness as the final images slip inside it, MUHAMMAD himself photographed in the variety of stress positions we've seen him in during the performance. The very last image is that of ABDELAZIZ's scalded face, spinning and laughing into oblivion. The projection goes dark and there remains the dim light on MUHAMMAD and ABDELAZIZ, in waltz position, as the voice of OUM KALTHOUM starts to sing. MUHAMMAD and ABDELAZIZ dance to the song as five or six new SOLDIERS with guns rush the stage in slow motion. They look obviously different from the previous soldiers, but unidentifiable, with ski masks and fatigues. The battle between the new soldiers and the original soldiers continues dramatically, all over the stage, using all previous locations, the INTERROGATION OFFICE, the SANCTUARY and the HOLDING CELL, as MUHAMMAD and ABDELAZIZ dance around them to OUM KALTHOUM's song until the soldiers, one by one, fall into each other's arms and start dancing too. They all spin and waltz on stage as the lights dim out and the voice fades out as well.

BLACKOUT.

EPILOGUE:

The following text is projected for the audience to read.

Black site prisons, prisons that operate outside the remit of any local or international law, are in use by a number of politically significant countries including Russia, China and the United States.

Since 9/11, the U.S. has detained 780 Muslim men and boys that we know of, most of whom have never been charged with a crime, and all of whom have been tortured.

At the time of this writing, 30 such detainees are still being held by the CIA in the Guantánamo Bay detention camp, Cuba.

The official term for these prisoners is "detainees," but there is no believable rationale which would stop us from calling them hostages.

In the darkness and the silence, the phone rings one more time.

THE END.

The Short Story

When the Phone Rang
by Youssef Alaoui

In the years between the wars, there was a prisoner. He had been plucked from the streets of his town because he was walking home with bread on the wrong day. Because the black smoke blew south rather than north. Because invading forces mistook themselves for rebel forces. Because rebel forces mistook themselves for allied forces. Because the crusaders were, in fact, supporters. Because a gunnery sergeant spoke like Yosemite Sam.

Because that sergeant howled and gesticulated from his perch, farting out last night's Spam chili in the back of a truck picking off *Hajjis* and then he shot a little boy, after the boy had shooed his sister home on her bicycle. The *because* didn't matter anymore. This prisoner had been detained in the same manner as any other enemy combatant, if they are not killed on sight.

It was well within the broad and permissive guidelines defining enemy combatants, as they are wont to flex and shake like the disco shorts of a midnight cowgirl, snapping gum and smiling on the phone behind the hotel bushes, under the stairwell of military protocol, commingling with bloodlust and prescription-addled shellshock.

The prisoner was named Muhammad. Muhammad had been chained to a concrete floor in a stress position for four days. This was the fifteenth such session in his broad career as a prisoner for the past four years. His knees felt like railroad pikes had been sledgehammered down through the marrow. His eyes felt like they wept blood, and his teeth were folding in on themselves, or maybe the entire thing was an illusion. The feeling was convincing enough to make him believe that he would never die. But that he would see heaven unfold before him, right there in his cell, shitting himself, chained to the floor, viewing it glow through his hood, to the tune of the music played through the speakers above. Inside that selfsame hood, he had carefully traced out the lines of tree-filled windows with his mind's eye.

His windows were dressed with blowing curtains and mounted in walls of flowery wallpaper. The ringing in his ears was birds chirping by day and crickets by night. He tapped his thighs in remembrance to the drumbeats of his youth, now burned and stamped out like rank cigarettes made of chewing gum paper, stuffed with camel dung.

Muhammad hated the invaders. He prayed for vengeance. He felt himself slowly dying in his cell. He called out in his brain to Allah to come visit and take him away. His mouth was no longer operating efficiently. He muttered and sobbed. He had no further hope of returning home. His new home was dark, but well-lit within the universe he had created. In this universe, his couch was soft. Thick with rugs. His record player worked.

His television was boring. Delightfully boring and irrelevant. He sat against the couch on the floor and gazed for hours at the shifting images on his black and white television set. Egyptian movies from the 1950s and 1960s streamed endlessly. Oum Kalthoum sang to full auditoriums with her arms out wide, sound emanating from her chest, the core of her love, as he dozed lightly, deep in the summery afternoons of the galaxy behind his black hood.

Corporeal pain was the last thing to tie Muhammad to this world. It confined him like a shipyard rope, tight against his midriff, squeezing out the final drops of his humanity. His tears would not spill forth. His eyes dripped something slowly, more viscous than tears, which he assumed was blood. The muscles in his face were also cramped and bleeding, for they were just as locked into a stress position as the rest of his body. The guards did not let him stand nor sleep, but he was removed from his cage daily for prayers and questioning. He had no ideas. He had no opinions. He knew a few people. Those people were doing their business. He did not want their business. He did want the guards dead and everything around him destroyed.

Muhammad lived his dwindling and meager life completely within the flowing drapes he had traced inside his hood. The hood was locked around his neck. His hands were chained to another chain that fixed his ankles to the floor, thus forcing him to crouch, forever. He kept his eyes on his windows. He watched the trees move beyond them. He saw birds and clouds passing. He had a prayer rug rolled up against the eastern wall. He turned on the television. Then the phone rang. He let it ring. *This phone doesn't ring*, he thought. *How can it?* The phone stopped ringing. He watched the undulating shapes of black and gray move in and out among the various dramas broadcast on his modest television. Late afternoon soon arrived. It was the hour of his nap. The phone rang. He picked it up.

He heard a tone. *Bip bip boop bip boop boop boop.* Couldn't be. It sounded like Morse code. He hung up the phone.

He remembered Morse code. He had studied it in school. It was a fascination for him for a while, a compulsion where, as he listened to his favorite music, he would try to match the lyrics spelled out in Morse code to the rhythm of the song by clacking his teeth softly inside his closed mouth, which rarely worked. Except for the occasional American Delta blues, to interesting effect. The message on the telephone must be expressly for him. But who would call him on his imaginary phone? It must be God. He should answer the phone and listen to the message of God—surely this was some kind of divine intervention. Maybe God was finally going to visit and thought he would be considerate enough to call first to clarify matters; perhaps there are conditions that he should know about. Any good scholar knows that God has plenty of conditions for pilgrims on their way to heaven.

Muhammad thanked his lucky stars and thought about the phone call for three days. He also changed the position of the phone. It had been on a table by the television, but instead, he moved it closer to the couch where he spent most of his time. That way, he could talk on the phone and gaze dreamily out the windows, or maybe talk about the programs he would be watching on the television. Yes, the phone would be closer so he could answer it quickly, perhaps by the first ring. Perhaps as the phone first starts to ring, like this:

Rrrrring

Hello! Yes, this is Muhammad! God? I have been waiting for so long to hear from you. Yes, I would be so overwhelmed with joy to live with you in your kingdom. Yes, I have kept to the five pillars. I have not yet made the Hajj. No, no cheating or lying. I am good to my fellow men. And women! I am kind to my mother! No, no masturbation. No. I am so sorry. That time was an accident.

Thank you for understanding, God. God, you are merciful! God, you are great!

The days spun on. The glee resulting from the prospect of receiving a telephone call from God built a tiny cabin in his soul, raising a puff of smoke from its chimney that made it easier for Muhammad to form words when he was brought in for questioning. Everything was better. The breeze in his sanctuary with the flowing curtains was always fresh and filled with light. The birds chirped calmly. The couch rose up to his ear for sweet dozing. His prayer rug was right where it had always been. His rug had a compass at the top.

Here, in this world traced inside his hood, the compass sometimes would spin for a few minutes. He would stare at it and try to feel the magnetic poles blowing past him like storm clouds, or maybe it was Mecca on a train car or, better yet, maybe the compass was stuck to the Kaaba which had escaped on a flying carpet to avoid the fundamentalists of the world, turning the compass around and around.

The phone rang again, once. He couldn't reach it in time. He picked it up anyway. *Hello?* No. He did hear a dial tone. He liked the sound of the dial tone. He listened until it stopped. Then he listened to the silence.

Muhammad pressed his finger on the button in the cradle of the telephone and it began to ring. He lifted his finger immediately.

Rrrrrr—
Hello!
Bip bip boop bip boop boop boop.
Sorry?
Boop boop bip bip boop.

Then nothing. He hung up. He thought about the combination of short and long pulses for the rest of the day. *Bip bip boop bip boop boop boop*, followed by *boop boop bip bip boop*. So odd. He thought to himself in

Morse code. He spelled out every thought, every concept, everything that entered his mind for that afternoon in Morse code. It took him the entire following day to correctly spell his thoughts on the matter. He gazed at himself in the bathroom mirror. He bowed and rinsed his face. *Boop boop bip bip boop*, he thought. Then, the inkling of an understanding edged in upon him. *No. Couldn't be! How silly. This is how God chooses to communicate?*

Muhammad laughed to himself and rinsed his face again. He walked back to the couch and grabbed a pen and some paper. He wrote down what the code meant:

Kif 7alik shu 3am ta3mil - (Howzzit goin wussup).

Allah speaks Arabish text slang crap? How could this be? Muhammad was on high alert. He couldn't believe it. Had he heard the code correctly? He was determined to find out. He placed the pad and pen next to the phone. The guards picked him up for questioning. He wouldn't speak. They soaked him in his hood. He imagined rain pouring down his windows. He gasped and gurgled. He couldn't believe what he had written. Could God be playing a trick on him? Perhaps this is a part of his torture. Somehow, the guards had found a way to enter his sanctuary. Muhammad wished for death. He no longer wished to be visited by God. The last thing he needed was to be visited by an asshole prison guard dressed up like God, if that could possibly be done. But if they were faking God, then why not fake godly speaking? Why would Allah choose to communicate with him in that Arabish text slang crap?

Muhammad sat and watched the television, dozing mindlessly for a long time. He practiced breathing slowly, so slowly, almost not breathing at all. He held tight to his jumpsuit. He felt the fabric against his skin. He became aware of the sandals wrapping his feet. He felt his breath entering the duct in his hood. He closed his eyes almost all the way. The curtains moved gently by the windows. Then, suddenly, he noticed a face slowly rising outside the near window. It had a mostly bald forehead with one long wisp of hair, moving with the breeze. It was the head of a man. The man had been seriously charred on the head. He was not balding—this was all that was left. Parts of his skull shone through his skin. One eye was missing. Most of his nose was missing. The man smiled, but then, half of his face was gone. His teeth were exposed. He couldn't help but smile. Muhammad's heart leapt out of his shirt. He felt his hood fly off his head. He lost track of his breathing. The hood hadn't actually gone anywhere, so Muhammad began to suffocate. He forced the words, "What the devil!"

"No. Not the devil," said the stranger, and he went away.

This couldn't have been a trick. The guards did not have the wherewithal to enter his mind in such a manner. Really, it was obviously some sort of trick, but nothing like he had ever experienced before in his exhaustive prison career. Could there have been a drug in the water they used on him the other day? Was that yesterday or two days ago? He couldn't remember. Maybe it was three days ago. Muhammad shook his head a few times. He tried to become present in his prison cell. He tried to remember what his cage felt like, what it smelled like. It became difficult to remember. Inside his sanctuary, he took the stress position of his physical body. It was very painful. He couldn't manage it for longer than five minutes. He had to rest. There was no way to sleep it off. The man in the window stated clearly that he was not the devil. But the devil is known to lie.

Then, the phone rang. Muhammad did not want to pick it up. It rang for five minutes. Then it rang again for an hour. Then the phone rang for the rest of the day. Muhammad's brain, his sweet and soft brain that had held up so well for four years of punishment, was now finding that its supporting timbers were no more than wet rags at the core. The entire structure of his elaborate, life-giving scaffolding began to rot into a stew; a tagine made of rifle butts and missile tips, bullet holes and jail bars, a concoction soaked with anger, resentment and hatred. At last, he answered the phone.

Hello?
Bip bip boop bip boop boop boop.
Noooo…no no no no no no no!

Muhammad heard light breathing. He was very quiet. He pressed the receiver more tightly against his head, pouring his ear down into the wires that might lead him out of prison, somewhere, somehow.

The voice took another breath. *You chased me away.*

Muhammad was stunned. He had no idea how to respond. He said,

I did not chase you away!
You called me the devil. You looked at me like I am some kind of madman. Who do you think you are, anyway?
You are not the devil?
No.
Aaaallah?

Muhammad's eyebrows raised up to his forehead and his forehead raised all the way back to his ears. He crammed the phone further against his ear, listening to the line so carefully, it was as if he could now hear the distant chatter of all telephone telemetry across the circuits for thousands of miles.

Certainly not.

Question marks bounded out of Muhammad's skull in every which way. He was now so afraid and yet so fascinated that it tripped his psychological governor, and he lost consciousness altogether.

The guards found him shortly thereafter and doused him with water. They allowed him to sit on the floor with his pants on. They brought him some hummus. He felt much more comfortable. They brought him some water. He sat in silence. The guards lowered the volume of the music. It played less often. Muhammad had the chance to think it all through a little better. Chased him away? He had done no such thing. Who was that, why wouldn't he knock? Why was his head so badly scalded? Did he need medical attention? Does he need a place to sleep? But just a second here, this was Muhammad's sanctuary, inside his head, and now there was a visitor, not just a visitor, but a Peeping Tom, a half-exploded Peeping Tom...and maybe even an enemy spy.

An enemy spy? Muhammad had no enemies. No political enemies, anyway. He sold shoes and used watches at the souk on weekends, before he was detained. That old bastard, Ali, down at the end of the lane was quite the boorish ass thought—but bless his soul, he might have made it out of town or was probably dead, *hamdoullah*, by the grace of God, but not this god. This was no god. This was a character who seemed to want to talk, despite his grisly appearance. Muhammad sat on the couch and alternated his attention between his television and the sunlight playing in the curtains. He fell deeply asleep.

He was awakened by the telephone. He felt the first ring internally, deep in his core, like a gurgling. The second ring began by shaking itself free of his innards, then it bubbled through his veins. The third ring jangled his very skeleton. Every iteration of the sound wave poured into his bones and, from there, vibrated the cells of his body. The bell was as nerve-racking as a fire alarm, but there was no exit available. The emergency was all the time, every day, every hour. No use for an alarm. He answered the phone on the fourth ring.

Yes.

Yes.

Do not play games with me, please.

This is no game.

Please tell me what you want from me. I have told the guards all that I know. Are you working for them?

By no means am I working for them.

What can I do for you, in the name of Allah, blessed be?

I am here to help.

Who are you? An angel? Are you Gabriel?

I am many things. I am a prisoner, like you. I was in Auschwitz. I was in the reeducation camps of Vietnam, of China. I have been in the places that have terror scarred into their name. Dubrava. Abu Ghraib. Guantánamo.

How?

I am you. I am your pain. I am The Pain. You may call me Abdelaziz.

How did you manage to get locked up in so many prisons?

Think about it some more.

I don't know what to think. (*The phone went silent.*) Hello?

Muhammad had no idea what all this meant. If he had been fed a hallucinogen four or five days ago, it surely would have left his system by now. Nothing else mattered. He had to know more. Who was this voice? How could he possibly speak without half a face? But, of course, this was a concoction of his own making. He had lined the inside of his hood with windows and curtains of his design. The phone was his creation. Of course. Muhammad had invented his world, he lived in it, he found sanctuary there and now there was an invader! With a story to tell, perhaps? Perhaps he could answer questions. Muhammad was too tired to ask any questions, and the soldiers had already asked *him* all the questions he could possibly answer. He was an empty husk.

A few days later, the telephone rang. Muhammad was ready. He was also more relaxed and prepared.

Hey-lo.
Yes.
Yes what?
Today I have called to tell you that these guards are not the enemy.
Oh.
Yes. You are to hold them in your heart from now on as if they were your brothers.
No.
Yes.
Who is this?
Abdelaziz. I have told you my name.
Are you a soldier? Are you with them? Are you the commanding officer?
Not at all. I am here with you.
So the soldiers are my brothers, their rifles scratch my back, and the bombs, they are my toys?
Ha-ha.

"Ha-ha"? Just what do you mean by "ha-ha"? Can you get me out of here?

Maybe. We might have to wait a bit longer.

Wait for what? Wait for them to run out of ammunition? Wait for them to run out of their despicable manners? Wait for them to run out of the will to control me?

Please relax.

Why should I relax when my life is spiraling down the drain? When it is a risk to my life to walk home with bread while being Arabic? Why should I relax when it is forbidden to go here or there while being from somewhere else? Why must I live my life out in this cage because of racial profiling, because of someone else's paranoid determination?

They act like that because they are scared. They are terrified.

Oh yes, of course. Because I said "BOO" and they are all now afraid. This is the most terrifying sound I can make:

BOOOOOOO!!!!

This is the sound of two cultures interfacing. When commerce is no longer sufficient, battles ensue. The cultures collide. Your conservatives versus their conservatives. Trust me. They are compassionate people. They are fascinated by the sound of your language and are also disgusted by it. They fear the sound of your vowels. Your ayin. *Your* qoph. *They know it is beautiful and yet still they hate it. They find it repulsive. They find your culture revolting yet fascinating. They think about you often.* How can you allow your women to dress like that? How can you run your business like that? How can you waste your natural resources like that? *It is strange to them and yet, they want to own it. They want to do your things for you, to correct your wrongs. In the same way, your culture finds their culture atrocious and invasive. Their culture is strange to you and your people. You wish they would stop. You think they are silly. You like their food. They think your food is weird. You want to be in Hollywood with their women. With their women's breasts. With their G-strings and bikinis. With their soft white children, swimming in purified blue pools.*

Muhammad could not believe what he was hearing. He loved the sound of his own language.

Their language is void of all meaning! It sounds like someone is kicking the stomach of a dying pig in heat! Ours is the language of God! Our writing is holy! Our calligraphy! They have nothing like that! And why in the name of God did you choose to contact me in Arabish? That mongrel savage language!
You used to speak it quite often.
What! Me? No!
To that woman in the burqa with her breasts out. You would ogle. She would chat with you and take your money.
Oh! No, I just happened to find her website. My friend showed me one day. Anyway, I stopped that! Never mind that! She was evil!
Arabish is the perfect language for you. It represents your base desires, everything that you

hate yet still fascinates you. This is the source of hatred. Fixation. Kissing cousins. Objectification, power, resistance. So fragile, so close, so disgusted by one another, and yet so attracted.

She was a wretched bitch! She took my money for nothing! She was probably in league with the conservative assholes to make a mockery of people like me, the average ones, the moderates! We are ready to live in a modern world! Stuck in the middle of politics and war! Victimized by every side!

Enough insults. They believe they are protecting the world.

From what? For whom? Okay, tell me what does it mean when they kill our children and bomb a hospital?

Why did the chicken cross the road?

Is that supposed to be funny?

Think about it. What does it mean?

What does what mean?

They bomb because it is in their nature. There is no answer. There are a million answers.

Oh, then there should be an all-out condemnation of Israelis, Jews, Arabs, Palestinians, Greeks, Turks, Russians, every single better-than-thou American...who am I leaving out? They all throw bombs!

And they all receive bombs. Why don't you tell me: what does it say about their nature when they kill children and bomb a hospital?

Because if it is in their nature, then it is not about options or politics—it is about their evil nature.

Bombs are built to kill humans. Bombs have one single function.

Bombs don't kill people. People do.

Bombs are just bombs. But more importantly, why do people keep building bombs and launching them at other people? Think about why they do it. Please.

I am not talking about people, I am talking about nations! I am not being metaphysical. I am not playing your game.

Neither am I. Bombs are built to kill and destroy. End of story.

So you are saying they are killers. That it is in their nature to be killers.

As are you.

I am not talking about our nation.

Not all of their nation are killers. And not all of your nation are killers.

I am talking about the children in the playground and at the hospital. They die playing on the beach. They die by the side of the road.

I am specifically talking about the warmongers. People are perversely fascinated by charnel. These nations did not take a consensus or vote together to determine where the next bomb would land. There is one man who made that choice.

Oh, I thought they were a democracy.

War is never a democracy. Peace is perhaps a democracy. At least it feigns democracy. War, a totalitarianism, is sold to Democracy as a temporary "minimal risk/maximum profit" endeavor. The heads of nations convince their public that the bomb attacks are guaranteed to be clean strikes. Backed by cold science. They call their bomb strikes surgical. Don't you get it? Surgical. That's why they aim at hospitals.

Now that was a joke.

Busted.

And what of the burned baby held by a crying man in a crowded funeral procession? How am I supposed to process this?

If you process it, you are involved in the war.

It is unavoidable, the violence is everywhere. In the streets. Film. Photographs. Right before my eyes! So what should I do, slash my wrists?

If you slash your wrists, you are participating in the exchange of violence.

I don't understand that. My life doesn't belong to you or anyone else. I don't agree with that assessment at all.

We are locked in a crisis of revenge. Cause and effect.

Okay, well then, I guess I can go shopping now.

Rather than react violently to the violent emotional exchange, we must accept and say, "The violence stops with me," rather than "The violence begins with me," or "The violence will

be continued by me." Or how about the following: rather than dropping bombs, these nations should get in a bus, drive over to the border of their enemy, ask permission to enter, be allowed to enter and let's say they sit themselves down in a hospital. Then they would gather the people and say to them: "Who among you will slash your wrists, because we are very angry! Not all of us here, but most of us are quite angry. Frankly, a few of us would rather be at home right now, but our bosses, who couldn't make it on this trip, have ordered us to come here to demand that you slash your wrists because our God is great, and we now own your land. Or else, we will do it for you. Even though we are not a hundred percent interested in slashing your wrists. A few of us would like to, however. About ten of us. Because we would like to get you back for that attack last week. No, it doesn't matter who suffers for our retribution. So who will step forward? Show us your babies!"
Show us your boobies?
Ha-ha.

You say nothing about processing your own emotions.
My emotions were burned away long ago. Here is what I say: the violence stops with me.

Abdelaziz had stopped talking. Muhammad kept listening to the empty line. Then he listened to the dial tone. Then he listened to the empty line again. He imagined a hundred thousand arguments coming to him through the wire. He imagined the violence and the retribution. He imagined the endless cycle of the violence whirlpool. He imagined a whirlpool so wide that the foaming sides were taller than the walls of a city, with trucks, guns and missiles thrown into the fray with entire hospitals, with women in burqas, with women in bikinis, with tattooed muscle men imprisoning and raping and beating them, with tattooed muscle men imprisoning and raping and beating each other, eating chili cheese fries smothered in hummus and olives, drenched in crude oil, covered in blood, getting shot for driving, getting shot for running, getting shot for minding their own business, getting shot for believing, for getting imprisoned, for getting caught forgetting where to be found in accordance with the law, with the Koran, with the Bible, with the Haftorah, for speaking the wrong language at the wrong time, on the wrong street corner, in the wrong country.

He imagined a giant spinning whirlpool with a tiny, pointed tip at the bottom that was so far down, so empty, so void of any mass, of any reason, of any conviction, a negative space so absorbing, so compelling that any mortal would be forced to dive toward it should one witness it, the eye of the storm, the crux of the void, so negative and hollow that there would always be room for one more to fill it.

That was what Muhammad's conversation with Abdelaziz had left him with. He was convinced that, under no circumstances, from now on, should he ever answer the telephone. He ripped the cord out of the wall decorated with flowery wallpaper. Then, he concentrated with all his might to erase the potentiality of another phone to reappear.

He went through every permutation he could fathom, should a telephone be delivered to his porch, or should one somehow assemble itself over the period of several days in his tool closet, or should any screws or wire scraps in his kitchen drawer randomly amount to the equivalent of a telephone.

Muhammad's prison sentence lasted another full year, maybe more. He enjoyed his painful silence. Eventually, he heard machine-gun fire and grenades at the main gate. Then, they were outside his building. Then, more down the hall, and then, finally, the guns arrived at his cage.

Afterword
A Note on the Adaptation by Anton Bonnici

As soon as I finished reading Youssef's short story, "When the Phone Rang," I knew that I had just experienced something of great potency, something that was reaching further, almost bursting out already, off the pages it was printed on. The first thing that one might gravitate towards is the tragic drama of the protagonist, the injustice, the inhuman treatment, the psychological warfare; these are all tremendously impactful realities brilliantly portrayed through the characters and conversations.

The stage gives us an opportunity to flesh out the interrogations even further and expose the degrading line of questioning to its full extent. By referring directly to the now publicly available CIA interrogation manual used in the aftermath of 9/11, I could recreate scenes which, unfortunately, might come quite close to the lived experience. Yet, there was something else that held my attention and made me feel the unrestrainable nature of this work, made me see it come to life in more extravagant ways than on paper…and that was its geography.

Space is a very real presence in this story. Everything happens in a specific space, and each specific space brings a new form of oppression or liberation, whether it's the interrogation room Muhammad is being questioned in, the cage he is being held and tortured in or the mental space where he is finding his refuge, a sanctuary.

It is these three spaces that made me immediately see this story happening on a stage. Three very distinct spaces happening practically simultaneously, one superimposed onto the other, one giving respite from the other, but, ultimately, each one might end up being even worse. Though some are physical and others mental, all these spaces are unreal. Spaces that should not exist in real life (and, for most of us, do not). Spaces that have been created as a side effect of one of humanity's very worst aspects: warfare.

What if we could show these spaces to those that might not have considered their existence? What if we could give a taste, even if within some modicum of safety, to those of us that have never been anywhere near such spaces? Might this not trigger some form of angry disapproval, some form of human rage, against the existence of such spaces? Might this not make us want to find them and do our best to motivate those in power to eradicate them? Why should we still live in a world that creates spaces with the aim to render people inhuman? Though not entirely successful, as we may see even here, the struggle for even a shred of humanity lasts till the very end in the darkest of places. Still, it is our obligation, our moral duty even, to somehow bring those places into the light. And with them, the people trapped within.

Acknowledgements

"When The Phone Rang" was first published in *The Opiate, Vol. 17* (2019) and also in Alaoui's short story collection, *Fiercer Monsters*, available from Nomadic/Black Lawrence Press.

Youssef Alaoui is a versatile writer known for his explorations of oppression, racism and colonialism in his poetry, short fiction and screenplays. His works have garnered recognition through three Pushcart Prize nominations and have been published both nationally and internationally. Alaoui holds an MFA in Poetics from New College of California, San Francisco.

Anton Bonnici is a teacher, playwright and dramaturge who aims to infect the world with as much enthusiasm for impactful playwriting and theatre-making as humanly possible. Over the past three years, he has dedicated his creative efforts to developing the *Not Theatre* theory and practice in tandem with the *Writing for the Stage* courses. He has produced and directed performances in Paris, London and Moscow, and his plays *Yet So As By Fire*, *Quasar Love* and *Pornotopia* have been published by The Opiate Books.

www.ingramcontent.com/pod-product-compliance
Lightning Source LLC
LaVergne TN
LVHW032012070526
838202LV00059B/6417